T0380661

Lucy's
HolyLand Adventures

LUCY VILLALON

Copyright © 2018 Lucy Villalon.

All rights reserved. No part of this book may be used or reproduced by any means, graphic, electronic, or mechanical, including photocopying, recording, taping or by any information storage retrieval system without the written permission of the author except in the case of brief quotations embodied in critical articles and reviews.

https://shop.spreadshirt.com/holyland-shirts-souvenirs/

Scripture taken from the King James Version of the Bible.

This book is a work of non-fiction. Unless otherwise noted, the author and the publisher make no explicit guarantees as to the accuracy of the information contained in this book and in some cases, names of people and places have been altered to protect their privacy.

WestBow Press books may be ordered through booksellers or by contacting:

WestBow Press
A Division of Thomas Nelson & Zondervan
1663 Liberty Drive
Bloomington, IN 47403
www.westbowpress.com
1 (866) 928-1240

Because of the dynamic nature of the Internet, any web addresses or links contained in this book may have changed since publication and may no longer be valid. The views expressed in this work are solely those of the author and do not necessarily reflect the views of the publisher, and the publisher hereby disclaims any responsibility for them.

Any people depicted in stock imagery provided by Getty Images are models, and such images are being used for illustrative purposes only.
Certain stock imagery © Getty Images.

ISBN: 978-1-9736-4148-3 (sc)
ISBN: 978-1-9736-4149-0 (e)

Library of Congress Control Number: 2018911843

Print information available on the last page.

WestBow Press rev. date: 10/27/2018

WESTBOW
PRESS®
A DIVISION OF THOMAS NELSON
& ZONDERVAN

The Holy City that is the apple of God's eye.

[23]And what one nation in the earth is like thy people, even like Israel, whom God went to redeem for a people to himself, and to make him a name, and to do for you great things and terrible, for thy land, before thy people, which thou redeemedst to thee from Egypt, from the nations and their gods?
[24] For thou hast confirmed to thyself thy people Israel to be a people unto thee forever: and thou, LORD, art become their God.
2 Samuel 7:23-24 KJV

An ancient, but beautiful city.

Zion's Gate

4

Ancient Olive Tree

**Lucy stays 8 nights at a local Jerusalem hotel touring
the Holy City and local attractions.**

Beautiful view from hotel balcony of the Holy City

A view of the City where Jesus spent much time as a child, and a city where Jesus at the age of 12 prayed and taught.

Иисус, Иоанн, пресвятая дева Мария,
Спасите и сохраните нас!

Camel Rides in the City are so much fun!

Lucy visits Bethlehem, the City where Jesus was born. Christmas Day long ago, a star appeared in the sky when Jesus was born.

The Wisemen followed the Star and it led them to baby Jesus. The Wisemen brought many gifts to the Christ child. This child would grow up to be a King.

Mary, Jesus's mother, and Joseph later leave Bethlehem with baby Jesus.

Lucy visits a church in Bethlehem where it is said is the area where Jesus was born.

Lucy visits Capharnaum
Jesus healed many people in Capharnaum

Jesus walked the streets of Capharnaum helping many people. Jesus loves people and loves helping them.

<u>Lucy visits site where Jesus was imprisoned.</u>
Jesus came to teach us the truth. Many people
did not want to listen to Jesus.

Jesus came to earth to teach us the truth and lead us to Heaven.

LES OUTRAGES CHEZ CAIPHE

Jesus chose to suffer much for all the world. Jesus still loved
the world even when the world mistreated Him at times.

29

Jesus was willing to come to earth to save the world no matter what. Jesus suffered because He loves us.

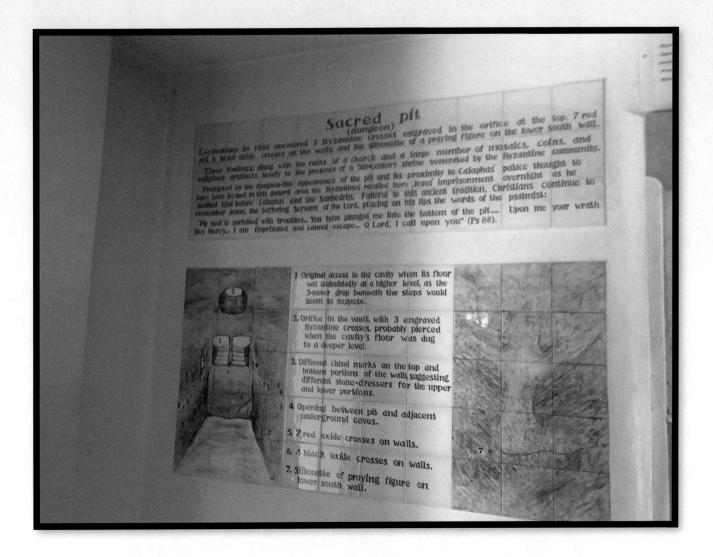

Sacred pit
(dungeon)

Excavations in 1889 uncovered 3 Byzantine crosses engraved in the orifice at the top, 7 red and 4 black oxide crosses on the walls and the silhouette of a praying figure on the lower south wall.

These findings, along with the ruins of a church and a large number of mosaics, coins, and religious artifacts, testify to the presence of a 5th-century shrine venerated by the Byzantine community.

Prompted by the dungeon-like appearance of the pit and its proximity to Caiaphas' palace thought to have been located in this general area, the Byzantines recalled here Jesus' imprisonment overnight as he awaited trial before Caiaphas and the Sanhedrin. Faithful to this ancient tradition, Christians continue to remember Jesus, the Suffering Servant of the Lord, placing on his lips the words of the psalmist:

"My soul is surfeited with troubles... You have plunged me into the bottom of the pit.... Upon me your wrath lies heavy... I am imprisoned and cannot escape... O Lord, I call upon you" (Ps 88).

1. Original access to the cavity when its floor was undoubtedly at a higher level, as the 3-meter drop beneath the steps would seem to suppose.

2. Orifice in the vault, with 3 engraved Byzantine crosses, probably pierced when the cavity's floor was dug to a deeper level.

3. Different chisel marks on the top and bottom portions of the walls, suggesting different stone-dressers for the upper and lower portions.

4. Opening between pit and adjacent underground caves.

5. 7 red oxide crosses on walls.

6. 4 black oxide crosses on walls.

7. Silhouette of praying figure on lower south wall.

Many people did not want to listen to Jesus and placed Him into a cave.

The prophets of old wrote about how Jesus would be treated.
Jesus was willing to go through much pain and suffering to
save the world. Jesus did this because He loved the world.

Even Jesus's friend Peter denied knowing Jesus.
Peter was fearful and denied Jesus three times.
Non Novi illum means: I don't even know Him.
Here is a statue of Peter denying he knows Jesus.

<u>Lucy visits the Garden Tomb</u>
The tomb where Jesus was buried. Jesus died for our sins.

Many beautiful gardens are located at the Garden tomb site.

45

Skull Hill is the location where Jesus was crucified.
The Hill has a form of a skull.
"And when they were come unto a place called
Golgotha, that is to say, a place of a skull"
Matthew 27:33 KJV

47

48

Jesus was taken off the cross by a man named Joseph. He was placed in a tomb in a cave.

"A man planted a vineyard. He put a wall around it, dug a pit for the winepress and built a watchtower."
Mark 12.1

Lucy and many people who love Jesus visit the tomb to remember what Jesus did for us. There are many beautiful gardens surrounding Jesus tomb that Lucy visited.

Jesus rose out of the tomb on the third day. Jesus is alive, well, and resurrected. It is finished.

Lighted/glowing Angelic being/wings captured on Lucy's camera while visiting Jesus tomb in Israel. Another tourist mentioned visibly seeing the Angelic wings.

**One of God's Holy angels declared that Jesus was not here- "for He is risen!"
"It is finished, mission accomplished."**

<u>Lucy visits MASADA</u>

Long ago, a King named Herod built a fortress, high on the
mountaintop, named MASADA, to hide. King Herod wanted
to stop Jesus from sharing His message of salvation.

**Herod is no longer there and now the site named Masada
visited by many. God's birds now live on the site.**

**Lucy visits the Jordan River- the River Jesus was baptised in.
Jesus wants everyone to receive Him as their Lord and Savior.
Once you receive Jesus each follower gets baptised.**

Many beautiful buildings and churches are located near the Jordan River.

Lucy visits the Sea of Galilee where Jesus walked on the water and performed many miracles.

72

Lucy visits the DEAD SEA.
Many people visit this wonderful Sea, and the mud and salt help people's skin become softer and make people feel better after dipping in this sea. No fish live in the Dead Sea. That's why it got its name- The Dead Sea. Lucy is overjoyed seeing all the people enjoying this Sea God provided. God is good.

Once the Sun sets at this beautiful site, people go home feeling better and ready for a good nights sleep.

<u>Lucy shops in the HolyLand.</u>
There are many beautiful things to buy to remind us of Jesus and
His HolyLand. Many things sold are carved from Olive Tree wood.

There are many stores with yummy treats in this Holy City.

Lucy loves to watch the people go by.

Many nice things sold to bring home and remind us of Jesus.

Lots of fun handbags and purses.

All sorts of nice things to buy.

Yummy loaves of bread to eat. JESUS is the bread of life.

The Sea of Galilee provides lots of fish for people to eat in the Holy City. When Jesus was in the Holy City He performed many miracles. Jesus was able to feed 4000 people with only a few fish. There is nothing impossible for Jesus or for those who believe in Him.

Jesus commanded us to be the fishers of men. If you don't know Jesus, I'll ask you to let Him into your heart right now. Say this prayer:

"Dear Jesus, thank you for coming to earth and dying on a cross for all the worlds sins. I'm sorry for my sins and want to receive you as my Lord and Saviour. I receive you right now into my heart."

Now go out and tell others you received Jesus and let them know about what Jesus did for them as well. Someday soon Jesus will return to make the world a better place.

That if thou shalt confess with thy mouth the Lord Jesus, and shalt believe in thine heart that God hath raised him from the dead, thou shalt be saved.
For with the heart man believeth unto righteousness; and with the mouth confession is made unto salvation.
Romans 10:9-10 KJV

To help share JESUS with others, or for HolyLand
shirts and souvenirs, visit Lucy's website:

https://shop.spreadshirt.com/holyland-shirts-souvenirs/

These shirts and souvenirs are great ways to break the ice to lead to
a conversation about JESUS and God's HolyLand message.

Printed in the United States
By Bookmasters